W9-DEZ-221

JOSEPH CONRAD

JOSEPH CONRAD : THE MAN

BY

ELBRIDGE L. ADAMS

A BURIAL IN KENT

BY

JOHN SHERIDAN ZELIE

Together with some Bibliographical Notes

HASKELL HOUSE PUBLISHERS LTD.

Publishers of Scarce Scholarly Books

NEW YORK. N. Y. 10012

1972

HASKELL HOUSE PUBLISHERS Ltd.

Publishers of Scarce Scholarly Books

280 LAFAYETTE STREET

NEW YORK, N. Y. 10012

Library of Congress Cataloging in Publication Data

Adams, Elbridge L   1866-
    Joseph Conrad.

    Includes bibliographical references.
    1. Conrad, Joseph, 1857-1924. I. Zelie, John
Sheridan, 1866-1942. A burial in Kent. 1972.
II. Title. III. Title: A burial in Kent.
PR6005.O4Z544   823'.9'12 [B]   72-2130
ISBN 0-8383-1487-2

Printed by *William Edwin Rudge*
Mount Vernon, New York.
485 copies, of which 450 are for sale.

Printed in the United States of America

Delaware Valley
College Library

23
763Yad

79-139

TO

JESSIE, BORYS and JOHN

Proud possessors of an immortal heritage

PREFACE

THE *longer of the two articles which make up this book appeared originally in "The Outlook" for April 18, 1923. It was written at the suggestion of the editor of that journal, who thought that the public should know more of the human side of an author who was fast becoming its literary idol; but it was not published without Mr. Conrad's consent. Indeed, so fearful was I of saying anything that might offend his sensitive nature and thus perhaps bring to ruin a happy friendship, that I took the precaution of sending him the manuscript with the request that he should dispose, delete, or even destroy, as it might please him. In returning the copy, he wrote: "I have just finished to annotate and modify as you permitted me to do. You may think I have been too meticulous in the alterations suggested. My view is that this first personal sketch by a friend of mine will become an authority. People will refer to it in the future. This accounts for my care to get the shades of my meaning established in your recollections, which are wonderfully accurate in the main."*

PREFACE

Here would seem to be a sufficient warrant for reprinting the article and for adding some extracts from Conrad's letters, which during his lifetime could not be made public without exceeding the limits imposed by good taste and good manners. These will reflect his attitude towards his visit to America, and will reveal the deep tenderness of his nature.

There is a melancholy satisfaction in being able to include in this book such a sympathetic account of Conrad's funeral as that of Mr. Zelie, who met Conrad when he was in this country in May, 1923; was captivated by his charm of personality and conversation and forthwith became his devoted admirer. It happened that Mr. Zelie was in Canterbury on the day when the dust of the great romanticist "was returned to the earth as it was," and so is able to reproduce vividly for us the scenes of that solemn home-coming.

I have thought it might be of interest to collectors of Conradiana to see the inscriptions written by Conrad in two sets of his works, and these are appended.

To Mr. Muirhead Bone my thanks are due for permission to use his masterly dry-point portrait of Conrad for the frontispiece.

JOSEPH CONRAD : THE MAN

BY

ELBRIDGE L. ADAMS

PREFACE

It is a pleasure to add that this book, in its design and printing, bears testimony to Mr. Bruce Rogers' own admiration for Conrad's art, and to him I make grateful acknowledgment of the care he has given to its production.

E. L. A.

JOSEPH CONRAD : THE MAN

Ever since I came upon "The Nigger of the Narcissus" in tranquil ante-bellum days I had been under the spell of Conrad's art. "Typhoon," "Lord Jim" and "Chance" were read with increasing beguilement, and then "Nostromo," that most astonishing creation of the imagination. One felt that here, indeed, was a magician who could conjure up the very spirit of some Eastern river and make one smell the rank stifling jungle or feel the motion of the ship as it drives before the hurricane. Nothing quite like these stories was to be found in the entire range of English literature. One was prepared to agree with Galsworthy that such writing "is probably the only writing of the last twelve years [he was referring to 1896–1908] that will enrich the English language to any great extent." But what sort of man, one won-

3

dered, was this master craftsman who used the English language with such a sure instinct for the beauty of words; whose art could create such atmosphere in the printed page as Turner or Homer Martin might put upon canvas? Could it be possible that he was a Pole, who had not known a word of English until he was twenty-one? The miracle deepened. One was ready to believe almost anything of such a prodigy; but there was so little to be learned about him. Beyond the fact that he was born in the Ukraine in 1857; that he went to sea when he was seventeen, in fulfillment of a resolution formed several years before and persisted in doggedly against all efforts of family and tutors to dislodge it; that he deliberately chose the red ensign of England as the flag he was to sail under, and that for twenty years "that symbolic, protecting, warm bit of bunting, flung wide upon the seas," was the only roof over his head; that during this hard and exacting life, through all its grades up to master in the merchant service, he had found time to learn the English language;[1] that finally, at the age of thirty-eight, he

1. Conrad wrote on the margin of my manuscript : "My dear, I arrived in England in '78 and I knew Eng-

had been invalided back to England, broken in health and with little capital for the succeeding years, save a wealth of experience and a first novel, which at once found a publisher; that ever since then he had lived apart from the busy life of London, somewhere in rural England, and that at intervals there had come from his pen romance after romance and story after story, until some twelve or fourteen books made up the sum of his literary achievements—beyond this meager outline of fact little was known to the public at large about Mr. Conrad. When an opportunity unexpectedly came in 1916 to meet him in the intimacy of his home life, through the introduction of a well-loved friend of his household, I embraced it eagerly.

The Conrads (one likes to speak of them in the plural, for Mrs. Conrad holds a place in the

lish in 1881, when I passed my examination for second officer during which I had to write a paper of so-called 'definitions' of navigational and other subjects which was not very difficult but demanded a certain knowledge of the language. I was helped by some general culture. In '74, when I went to sea, I had left the lower fifth of St. Anne's public school in Cracow. I was fit to take care of myself intellectually."

affections of her husband's friends that has not been shared by the wife of a man of literary genius since the days of the Brownings) were living at that time at Capel House, in Kent, a county in which Mr. Conrad had made his home for the greater part of the time since his marriage in 1896.

It was during the early part of September. The English army was just then making its greatest offensive in the battle of the Somme—an offensive which will forever be memorable because of the first appearance of those strange machines, shaped like monstrous toads, which crawled relentlessly over wire and trench and parapet, the British "tanks"—and the booming of the guns in Flanders could be heard across the Channel. Borys, the eldest son of the Conrads, was somewhere over there in the mud, getting his baptism of fire, and there had been no news of him for a fortnight. The life of an English officer of the line in that desperate time was calculated, actuarially, at some forty-odd days, and it was not surprising that the Conrads were filled with dread lest any moment of the day should bring ill tidings. Indeed, that very morning some neighbors of theirs had sent word that they had received the fateful

6

message from the War Office which had changed
their suspense into a grim but proud certainty.
This preoccupation gave a sombre tone to the
day and made the dispensing of hospitality something of an effort, I fancy. If so, it was well con-
cealed beneath a wealth of cordiality which, going
out primarily to the old friend of the family, embraced the guest in its generous welcome.

Conrad met us at the Ashford station and ran
us over to his moated farm in a Ford. Of medium height, distinguished in appearance, quick
and nervous in movement, he looked more like
an Englishman than I had envisaged him. But as
soon as he began to speak, though his speech was
not at all hard to understand, it was just strange
enough to make one aware that the speaker was
not of English blood. I thought him a little re-
served and severe in manner at first, but this
appearance of austerity wore off when we were
seated at the luncheon table. I did not know
then, what I came to learn five years later, that
Jessie Conrad was renowned in her intimate circle
for that homely but admirable art which was to
furnish occasion to her husband for the charming
preface to her "Simple Cooking Precepts for a

Little House," which has made a cookery book, for the first time, a literary as well as a culinary delight. What I did observe was that "the impeccable practice, which," Conrad graciously says, "has added to the sum of his daily happiness for more than fifteen years," made the conversation flow naturally and pleasantly around and across the table. Conrad was the urbane host, with none of the posings or affectations which are sometimes the pretensions of men of genius. The youngest son, John, then a boy of about ten, came to the table with a tale of some mechanical engine of war he had invented, and there were quips and jokes about the length of the war and as to whether John's contrivance would be in time to save civilization. This was the time when our English cousins were saying rather pointed things about Americans who were too proud to fight, but Conrad was much too tactful to indulge in gibes that might give offense to his guest. He did make some amusing references to one or two Americans whom he had met, but whom he very properly recognized as exceptions to type. They were of the kind who patronize men of genius without understanding them and were antagonistic to the deeper fineness of his nature. He spoke most admiringly of that true American, Walter Hines Page, then known by so few of his countrymen. They learned to appraise him truly after his death, when his letters revealed the nobility of his life and character as one of the greatest of ambassadors and patriots.

He also mentioned with much affection and enthusiasm an American author little remembered in this generation, but the possessor of an enduring fame—Stephen Crane, whose "Red Badge of Courage" was universally recognized when it appeared, in the closing years of the last century, as a work of genius. Conrad had been attracted to him, and he to Conrad, when he went to England to live after the Spanish War, and Conrad has immortalized their friendship in a little memoir which may be found in "Notes on Life and Letters."

Another American of whom Conrad spoke with feelings of great veneration was James Fenimore Cooper. He freely acknowledged his debt to this master of the English language, saying that Cooper's artistic instinct was genuine and unerring, though his style was that of the age in which he wrote, both in its beauties and its defects. "He did know the sea, its moods and its men, as few writers have known them, and in some passages of his novels he reached the very heights of inspiration," was Conrad's comment.

But it is with Henry James, then a few months dead, that Conrad has been thought to have the nearest kinship among English writers, and I was curious to know his opinion of him. At my question he pointed to a shelf of books which included the uniform selected edition and all the other works of the great American novelist which were not included in it. He said: "I loved him. He was most charmingly kind to me and my wife. He was a specialist in the art of creative literature, who dealt with the most delicate shades of emotion—the historian of fine consciences—and he was always master of his materials. He was the true artist, who creates because he must, and I read his books again and again with the deepest admiration. His place in English letters is secure."

It has been a matter of common knowledge that Henry James and Joseph Conrad had a profound admiration for the exquisite art of Turgenev. It seems to me that they are alike in this also—that each found something in the spirit of England and of its institutions which won his allegiance and veneration. I have noticed another similitude between them, of apparently trivial importance, and yet one of those traits which are sometimes the outward manifestation of great depth of character and conscience. The readers of Henry James's "Letters" will remember that it was his invariable custom when writing to a friend, by dictation, to apologize for making use of the typewriter—"this fierce legibility," as he called it. So Conrad, with the same sensitiveness and old-fashioned courtesy and high breeding, when he is compelled by the pain in his wrists, which he frequently suffers, to resort to a typed letter, always does so with contrition, as though it were the deadliest of social sins, and with a petition for forgiveness for such a departure from his high code. Even then he manages to take the curse off "the machine-made, impersonal thing" by a few closing paragraphs in his own fine, bold handwriting.

After luncheon, when the ladies had gone upstairs, Conrad took me to his study and, proffering me a box of what he called "real tobacco cigarettes kept exclusively for guests" while he took a war-time "grape-vine," "because they are what our boys in the trenches smoke," he said, rather abruptly: "I understand that you are collecting my first editions. What have you had to pay in America for some of them?" I mentioned some of the prices which his earlier books were bringing. He thought them absurdly high, and wondered that any one should be willing to pay them. He is temperamentally unable to understand the collector's point of view.

"And have you got everything I have published?"

"Yes, everything I know of," I replied.

"Have you the privately printed preface to 'The Nigger of the Narcissus'?"

No, I had not heard of it. He then told me that he had written that preface to express his intimate feelings about the aim of the art of fiction—"the appeal of one temperament to all the other innumerable temperaments, through the senses"—and that his publishers had suppressed it because it was deemed, at the time, inadvisable to print it with the novel. He wished, however, to preserve it, and caused a few score copies of the "Preface" to be struck off in pamphlet form, and distributed among his literary friends. It may now be found in all the editions of "The Nigger" in America, and should be read by those who would have a fuller understanding of Conrad's art. "You would better look it up when you get back to London," he said. "It is becoming quite scarce. A copy fetched ten pounds at auction the other day, I am told."

Conrad then asked: "Which of my books do you like the best?" " 'Some Reminiscences,' " I hazarded, not without hesitation, for I at once thought of "Typhoon." Conrad's face lighted up with unaffected pleasure. "Why, you surprise and please me not a little," he said. "That is not considered one of my popular works, and some of my literary friends have told me it was too unconventional and informal to be good autobiography, and too remote from English and American associations to be very interesting. I have always rather regarded it as a good piece of work and as a faithful record of the feelings and sensations connected with the writing of my first book, and with my first contact with the sea—a human document which would, to those who can see eye to eye, reveal the personality behind the books I have written. Perhaps it should not have been written at all; perhaps it is unimportant what sort of a human being the artist is; his art should speak for itself. But there was such a persistent demand from my little audience that I should raise the curtain and explain how it was that a Polish boy should become an English seaman, and then an English writer, that I could not, notwithstanding my doubts, resist the temptation to speak about myself."

It was then my turn to ask a question; and I suppose it was the same question that every admirer of Conrad's stories asks:

"How was it possible for you, a Pole, coming to England at the age of barely twenty, with no previous knowledge of the language, to write such idiomatic English prose, even in your first book?"

"I think I must have some talent for language," answered Conrad. "It is said to be a Polish aptitude. I learned French when 1 was quite young, and can speak it or write.it fluently now. I did not deliberately choose English as my medium of expression. It chose me. The ground was prepared by my reading of Shakespeare, Dickens,

and much other English literature in Polish trans-
lations. I knew not a word of English when I first
set foot on English soil. I read a good deal during
the years I followed the sea, and when I began to
write it came as natural for me to write English
as if it had been my own native tongue. I never
thought of expressing myself in French. English
seems to be a part of my blood and culture."

Then he asked me to take a little excursion
in the lovely Kentish country, and we went off
alone in the Ford to the top of a hill, from which
we looked down across the Romney Marsh. We
stopped in the little village of Ruckinge to ex-
amine the architecture of its Norman church,
and Conrad pointed out, with the enthusiasm of
an amateur, some of the Elizabethan restora-
tions and the particularly lovely painted glass
windows.

On the way home something by the wayside
—the deserted appearance of a public house, I
think it was—led me to say that England was
handling the problem of liquor traffic during the
war with a wise discrimination, and that it was
to be hoped she would continue to do so when
peace should come again. Immediately Conrad

was all excitement. It was as if a shell from one of those trans-Channel guns had burst at our feet. Did anything justify a restriction of the liberty of the individual to do as he liked, so long as he did not interfere with the liberty of any one else? What would become of the boasted freedom of Englishmen if such paternalism became the accepted policy of the English Government? I defended my position as well as I could; I cited the destitution of the workingmen in some parts of London and Glasgow as an evil which the State should correct; I suggested that England's pre-eminence as a trading nation after the war might be seriously jeopardized if drunkenness were not abated. But everything I said seemed to add fuel to the flames. The whole nature of the man —the Polish temperament, with its tradition of self-government and its exaggerated respect for individual rights—cried out against this infraction of his personal liberty. It was that liberty which had attracted him to England as the country of his adoption. It was the greatest possession England had given to the world. Could she be so false to her best traditions as to undertake to regulate by law the personal habits of her

16

people? He pointed out how, within his recollection, the English nation had been getting rapidly more and more sober by individual effort, by example, by force of character, without any legislation. As an illustration, he referred to the marked change in the character of ships' crews. At the end of his time at sea it was very rare to find one man coming to join a ship drunk, he said, whereas in his early days more than half of a crew of twenty would be more or less tipsy.

I felt, when we reached home, that I had unwittingly struck a false note that had marred the harmony of a delightful day. But the discord was to furnish the occasion for a charming incident. Mrs. Conrad, perhaps shrewdly suspecting the situation when she saw two rather tense men walk in at tea-time, sent her young son upstairs for a photograph of the house, which she gave me as a memento of the day, with many pretty speeches. This gave Conrad an opening. Waving his hand towards his wife, he said: "It is you, as usual, Jessie, who make the agreeable impression. 'What a charming woman Mrs. Conrad is,' our guest will say when he is on the train, 'and what a brute of a husband she has, to get so excited over nothing!" Then, as we all joined in the hearty laughter that followed this sally, John was again sent off to the upper room with some whispered directions, and returned with a package, which he handed to his father. Conrad sat down at his desk, and for a few minutes was busy with some writing. Then, turning around, he said to Mrs. Conrad, "There are only three copies of the 'Preface' to 'The Nigger of the Narcissus' left. These two I put in this drawer to be kept for our boys. The third I am going to give to our new friend, hoping that he will remember only the pleasant events of this day," at the same time handing me, inscribed with a note explaining its genesis and signed by him, what is one of my most treasured literary possessions.

It may be interesting to bibliophiles to know that a complete set of first editions of Conrad's books, including some scarce privately printed pamphlets, will bring, to-day, upwards of two thousand dollars. This, I believe, constitutes a record for any author in his own lifetime, within a quarter of a century after the publication of his first book.

As I went back to London that evening there remained with me the impression of a strong,

sane, virile, and extraordinarily vivid personality
—the personality of a man of delicate conscience,
of generous enthusiasms, and an intense regard
for the obligations imposed by honor; of deep
human affections and of great tenderness, tinged
with just a shade of the sadness that comes from
long association with the sea. Joseph Conrad,
perhaps through the hardships and suffering in-
separable from the life of a mariner, has achieved
a loftiness of character and a simple grandeur of
soul which, I think, are reflected in that epic
quality which is found in almost everything he
has written.

The friendship thus begun was kept warm by
an exchange of letters from time to time. In 1919,
when we in America were face to face with pro-
hibition as a National policy, I wrote to Conrad
confessing a change of mind. This drew from him
the following response:

"Your letter has made me feel ashamed again,
after the lapse of years, for the utterly unneces-
sary heat in argument which I displayed that
afternoon when you and I went for a drive in the
Ford and discussed the question of individual
liberty. I remember when I confessed it to my

wife, afterwards, with much compunction, how shocked she was. But you have been extremely good about it. Your candid letter was very pleasant reading for me, mainly because my point of view has become practically demonstrated to you. Pray do not believe that I am triumphing, for there is much to say for the other—I may call it the ethically utilitarian attitude. In fact, it is the undeniable strength of that attitude which makes it so exasperating to the objectors of my sort. The foundation of my argument was really the feeling that there is more than one kind of utility, whether in the moral or in the material sphere."

Two years later, when the world had fallen upon happier times, I met Mr. Conrad again. There had been some correspondence about a motor trip together through southern England, but in August, while M. and I were in Switzerland, word came from Conrad that an eminent London surgeon who had come down to see Mrs. Conrad had prescribed certain treatment for her lameness which made automobiling out of the question; but that they would be at home all summer and would expect to see us when we came to England.

THE MAN

On a radiant day in September, 1921, we motored down to Canterbury, and, after a hurried glance at the mother of English cathedrals, more inspiring than ever in its majestic Gothic choir (it seemed a strange reminder of the purpose of our pilgrimage that in the earlier Norman church, built by Lanfranc and Anselm, the choir had been known as "the glorious choir of Conrad"), we ran out to Bishopsbourne, the new home of the Conrads. This marked a great change in Conrad's worldly condition. His motor vehicle had kept pace with it. He said, whimsically, referring to the old Ford: "Now I have a Cadillac to keep the new house in countenance." The new house, of charming domestic architecture, is situated in the park belonging to Bourne Hall, and has a fine lawn and some remarkably handsome specimens of wide-spreading beech trees, which Conrad pointed out to us with much pride. He had been suffering fearfully from an attack of gout, his ancient enemy, but he was in excellent spirits, and, with almost boyish enthusiasm, carried off M. to see his three gardens, each a little different from the others and all full of natural loveliness.

When we had gained the seclusion of his study, after luncheon, I asked him if we might expect soon another romance from him. He said that the reaction from the war strain had inhibited, for the time, his creative mood after the finishing of "The Rescue," but that he was beginning to write again, and hoped to complete two novels which were stirring within him. (I have heard lately that he has finished one, and that the other is half written.) He spoke rather wistfully of his desire to see his affairs in good order before the years should put an end to his work, but hoped to die in harness.

"You must remember," he said, "that success came to me, in a material sense, only in 1913, after eighteen years of steady writing. Then came the war, checking the normal development of that material prosperity to a great extent and bringing calls on my resources—calls the strength of which one could not resist, and, indeed, never thought of resisting. Now, as my health does not grow more robust with the years, I must make the most of my time when I am able to work."

I urged him to think of coming to America, perhaps to give some lectures here, but he seemed to doubt if his health would permit such an undertaking.

"I have sailed all of the Seven Seas except the northern Atlantic Ocean, and I should dearly like to cross that before I die," he said, and added, with a poignant shrug, "but I am afraid my traveling days are over." And then, as if to indicate that he would like to entertain the thought of such a journey, he said, "Still, one can never tell."

He is deeply interested in the United States, its people, its Government, and the mighty development of a world power which is also a great democratic state. He spoke of the decision of the Supreme Court upholding the Eighteenth Amendment, and was disappointed that the Court had given no reasons for its decision. "Whatever they were," he said, "it only confirms my very early conviction that a representative government is but a poor guaranty of liberty. Yet I do not see what else we could put in the place of it. I am afraid that most human institutions are poor affairs at best, and that even a Heaven-sent constitution would not be safe from the distorting force of human passions, prejudices, hasty judgments, emotional impulses, or from mere plausible noise raised by an active and determined minority."

Though, like all good artists, Conrad is devoted to his art, he is not entirely preoccupied by it, but is a man of remarkably broad vision and sympathy. The following paragraph from a letter written shortly after the English elections of November, 1922, shows his philosophical grasp of political questions:

"We have just emerged here from the very moderate and indeed remarkably mild turmoil of a general election. The Labor Party has attained, by its numbers, to the dignity of being the official Opposition, which of course is a very significant fact and not a little interesting. I don't know that the advent of class parties into politics is abstractly good in itself. Class for me is, by definition, a hateful thing. The only class really worth consideration is the class of honest and able men, to whatever sphere of human activity they may belong—that is, the class of workers throughout the nation. There may be idle men; but such a thing as an idle class is not thinkable; it does not and cannot exist. But if class parties are to come into being (the very idea seems absurd), well, then, I am glad that this one had a considerable success at the elections. It will give to Englishmen who call themselves by that name (and among whom there is no lack of intelligence, ability, and honesty) that experience of the rudiments of statesmanship which will enable them to use their undeniable gifts to the best practical effect. For the same reason I am glad that they have not got the majority. Generally, I think that the composition of the House is good. The outstanding personalities are not so promising. The majority of them—to be frank about it—are somewhat worn out; therefore one looks forward with great interest to those unknown, yet who, before long, are bound to emerge."

Mr. Conrad's place in the starry firmament of English literature may not yet be fixed with any degree of finality, though it is certain to be a high one. James Huneker, who was one of the first in this country to perceive Conrad's genius as a creative writer,[1] originally thought he should be put

1. I wrote originally "writer of romance." Conrad struck this out and interlined "creative writer." In the margin he wrote, "I had a discussion with H. himself once and he admitted that creative artist was a better definition for me than romance writer."

in the company of Meredith, James, and Hardy. This opinion he afterwards revised, and, in a letter to a correspondent he said: "I did not place him high enough. Joseph Conrad makes the fifth of a quintet of the world's greatest writers of fiction—Flaubert, Turgenev, Tolstoy, and Dostoievski."[1]

Whether this dictum will be accepted as the world's verdict, Time, the great critic, alone can determine. One who does not pretend to critical judgment may question whether Conrad has anything in common with the great Russian mystics, Tolstoy and Dostoievski. I know, from what I have heard him say, that he regards them as representing the negation of the austere virtues that he stands for—character, honor, duty, fidelity. Conrad looks upon life with the instincts and prepossessions of a Western mind.

But of the rightness of another opinion of Mr. Huneker's I think there can be no doubt. Writing from London in 1916 about the leading men in

1. Conrad's comment on this was "Dear Huneker had Russians on the brain. Tolstoy and Dostoievski deny everything for which I stand. I hate to hear my name pronounced in the same breath with theirs. To be classed with Flaubert is, of course, a great compliment."

the world of contemporary letters, he said: "J. C. is the most lovable of them all."

This sketch will have been written in vain if it shall fail to reinforce that judgment.

February, 1923

THE AMERICAN VISIT

In May, 1923, Joseph Conrad came to the United States. I might fill many pages with an account of this visit, but nothing I could say would have half of the interest, nor any of the charm which Conrad's letters will have for those who would know more of the human side of that strange genius. So I shall bring this sketch of Conrad the man to a close by giving some extracts from his letters to me, covering the period from December, 1922, to June, 1924, connecting them and explaining them wherever necessary by a few words of my own. In November, 1922, I wrote to tell him that I had seen an agent here who would offer him an attractive contract for a lecture tour of the eastern part of the United States in the following spring. In December there came the glad news that he was considering the matter seriously. "I will tell you in confidence," he wrote, "that my health and the state of my work permitting, I may come over to your side at the beginning of May. . . As a consequence of your letter of November 4th, F. N. D. [his American publisher], Pinker [his literary agent] and I. have been discussing the possibility of delivering some private lectures during that time. My health and perhaps my temperament could not stand a regular course under the direction of a manager in the usual way. Your opinion, however, that a visit from me would produce a good effect on the sales of my books, had enough weight with me to induce me to consider the above plan. I don't go into details but you can see from what I have said what it may be like. What do you think of it? I still have my doubts." There was of course, only one answer to that question and it went by return post.

The next two letters from Conrad contain paragraphs which show how supersensitive he was, and how he shrank from the ordeal of meeting strangers. "I beg you, my dear friend," he wrote, "do not plan engagements for me. Apart from the general uncertainty of human purposes, I do really believe that I may not be equal to it. Consider the effect of such novel experience on a man of my age, whose life has been hard and whose nervous system was always highly strung up, and the emotional side untried and unblunted, while the sensibilities have been exacerbated by many years of creative work in almost complete solitude, and don't be annoyed with me. If I had not been what I am it is very probable I would not have produced the writings that are before the public and contain the best that is in me. . . . I am hard at work on a novel ['The Rover'] and am feeling very well, but the uncertainty of which I have spoken prevents me from indulging in hopes. Even my *good* health is a very poor and precarious thing. What frightens me most is the fact that people on your side won't be able to understand how the commonest social exertion may, on any given day, be too much for me, and take my shrinking for ungraciousness, or laziness, or lack of appreciation, or any other repulsive trait of character."

In a later letter he said: "I can now tell you that short of buying the ticket, which I will do next Monday, I have made my arrangements to arrive at New York by the *Tuscania*, leaving Glasgow on April 21st. Pray don't mention this fact, because I want to keep the exact day of arrival dark. I imagine it will be the first or second of May. I will ask the Company to keep my name out of the passenger list and Doubleday has promised to be at the wharf to meet me and whisk me away. I take your own view of the visit to your side. I always shrank from considering it as a dollar-gathering expedition. I assure you that half of its significance would be gone for me if I were not to spend a day at least under your roof. Pray give my affectionate remembrance to Mrs. Adams."

And then he came!

I realized the moment I saw him descending the gangplank of the *Tuscania* that he was not well. He looked tired and harassed—even frightened—by the ordeal of running the gauntlet of ship reporters, Polish delegations and other curious and inquiring people. I had a few moments with him before he was "whisked away" by his publisher, who was to be his host during his short stay in America. He said: "Please tell your wife that I shall come to-morrow to pay her my respects." That was so characteristic of his gallant nature! He came the next day at tea-time. He was in high spirits and entered with zest into the arrangement, which was then made, for a visit at our summer home in the Berkshire Hills of Massachusetts on his return from a motor trip to Boston, Cambridge and Concord.

This visit came at the end of May. He dropped out of a motor car late one afternoon, stretched himself and said: "I am so glad your house is not white with green shutters. America to me has been one long line of white houses with green blinds."

He was a charming guest, always ready for a chat, or some music or whatever was suggested, except a walk or anything requiring physical exertion. The local newspapers would have it that he made pious pilgrimages to the homes or the haunts of Herman Melville, William Cullen Bryant and other literary celebrities. As a matter of fact, he never stirred farther from the house than the front terrace, to get the view of Mt. Everett

31

to the southwest or of Tom Ball Mountain to the north, the latter having as he thought a distinctly Italian aspect. He preferred to sit before the fire and play with the child of the house, smoking incessantly the French cigarettes which he liked, and of which my wife, who had remembered his taste, had laid in a store to his great delight.

We saw that he was tired and did not want to meet strangers and we guarded him against all intrusion. Muirhead Bone, who had come over on the *Tuscania* with him, arrived the next day, and while Conrad was in the music room listening in a rapt mood to the playing of some Brahms, Bone stole in with a large copper plate and made, in rather less than an hour, the dry-point portrait which has been reproduced as the frontispiece to this volume.

Dr. Zelie, who had long been an admirer of Conrad's art, dropped in one evening for dinner, and engaged Conrad in a conversation about some of his books. But for the most part his talk was of the homely, familiar things of life: of gardens and cooking; of children and the way to educate them; of the current happenings of the day, as to all of which Conrad seemed to be *au courant*.

And then, when we were beginning to think that we should like to have him stay on forever, and he had proposed to take a lease of the little cottage in the garden and pay "two radishes a year" as rental, his car came and took him away, and we saw him no more.

He sent us a charming letter of farewell, on the eve of sailing:

"I am ashamed of not having written to you and your dear wife before. I put it off from day to day in the hope of finding a really 'free' moment in which I could attempt to express to you my gratitude for your gift of warm friendship and charming hospitality. But that hope must be given up. Even now I am oppressed by the prospect of a dozen or more of letters to write— and by the packing which has to be done to-day.

"So a short word of thanks must do; and I put into its accent all the depth of sincerity which it can carry in its six letters. May the blessings of peace and contentment attend the life of comparative retirement which you intend to lead, and extend to your posterity of which Ann is such a lovely and lovable representative. I beg Margery to give her a kiss from me.

"I shall try to give Jessie some idea of your delightful home and its rural surroundings.

"If you ever have photos taken of your abode please send them to us for our American album. We shall look forward to important good news from you before long. I must ask you to send me a copy of the pamphlet when it appears, signed by you, for deposition in the family archives, so that my descendants should have this record of our friendship and of your views of me, and transmit it to their posterity.

"I am going away with a strong impression of American large-heartedness and generosity. I have not for a moment felt like a stranger in this great country about the future of which no sensible man would dare to speculate. But no sensible man would doubt its significance in the history of mankind. I am proud to have had from it an unexpected warmth of public recognition and the gift of precious private friendships. I kiss Margery's hands and grasp both yours in farewell and recommend myself and all mine to your kind and unfailing memory. Your affectionate and grateful friend

JOSEPH CONRAD."

There was a long interval after that when we heard from him only through Mrs. Conrad, and then nothing but rather dubious reports of his health. Finally, in March, 1924, came a letter full of tenderness, and foreshadowing the end. He said:

"Pardon me all my shortcomings. I am about the most imperfect man on earth; and if it had not been for the indulgence of my friends I would not know where to hide my head.

"The fact of the matter is, my dear friend, that all this year—up to 3 weeks ago—I have not been well at all. Now I am better and am doing some work, slowly. Mentally I feel still languid. But all this is improving.

"Epstein has been here for the last week doing my bust: just head and shoulders. It is really a magnificent piece of work. He will be done modelling this week and there will be five bronze copies cast. Muirhead Bone has arranged this. I was reluctant to sit but I must say that now I am glad the thing has come off. It is nice to be passed to posterity in this monumental and impressive rendering.

"Besides this there is not much news to tell

you. Alas! There is no chance of us coming to Mass. to take possession of the cottage. In September we will leave this house and go into winter quarters in the South of France—I hope. But Jessie is not getting on very well and we may have to stick somewhere near the surgeons for God knows how long.

"She is writing to-day to Mrs. Adams to whom please give my love, as well as to the chicks. Whatever happens keep me in your memory and believe me always yours

JOSEPH CONRAD."

And then in June there came another letter— the last—which shows plainly enough that the tired body was near exhaustion, though the spirit was still undaunted. The "typescript" referred to in the beginning of the letter was an article which Dr. Zelie had written about Conrad and asked me to send to him.

"We were very glad to hear from you and to know that you are all well and flourishing in the Green River Farm.

"I return the fifteen pages typescript with some remarks and slight corrections on the margins. My having done so is a sufficient definition of my attitude towards the proposed publication. The decision of course must rest with you. I have the best recollection of the personality of the writer, but a rather faint one of what was said on that particular evening. This does not mean that the memory of my visit to your home is a fading memory. That will never fade; for it is based on the warm and abiding sense of your and your wife's affectionate welcome and deep kindness, which surpassed my confident expectation and secured my lifelong gratitude.

"I suppose Jessie has written to your wife about the operation hanging over her head. Its date has been now fixed for the 13th of this month. We all, here, are hoping for the best; and indeed there are grounds to hope that it may finally do away with those painful local troubles which have disabled her and caused her so much suffering in the last two years. But of course one can't help being anxious.

"I haven't done much since you have seen me, and, truth to tell, I have not been very well either. Our intention is to leave this house in September, but I must confess that we have not yet found another. All this is very disturbing mentally—

and the sense of bodily discomfort of which I am almost never free is not very helpful to literary composition. I will not deny that my spirits suffer from this state of affairs. But I won't enlarge on that, which I regard as a passing phase which must be faced with all the resolution one can muster. . . ."

Joseph Conrad died at Bishopsbourne on August 3rd, 1924. He was weary and it was time for him to rest. He had worked up to the very last and so had realized his wish to die in harness. His own words from "The Mirror of the Sea" come to mind: "There is something fine in the sudden passing away of these hearts from the extremity of struggle and stress and tremendous uproar —from the vast, unrestful rage of the surface to the profound peace of the depths, sleeping untroubled since the beginning of the ages."

These lines of Spenser, which form the motto of the title-page of "The Rover," are carved on the stone which marks his grave in Canterbury cemetery:

Sleep after toyle, port after stormie seas;
Ease after warre, death after life, doth greatly please.

A BURIAL IN KENT

BY

JOHN SHERIDAN ZELIE

A BURIAL IN KENT

I⊤ was cricket-week in Canterbury and the
streets of the Kentish capital were gay with ban-
ners and alive with crowds. Hosts of visitors were
steadily streaming into the cathedral, where no-
body by any possibility can ever be disappointed.
If one were compelled to content himself with
just one cathedral he could not do better than
choose Canterbury. But there was no outward
sign anywhere that on that particular day of
August there was to be laid to rest in the ancient
city one who was almost England's first man of
letters, Joseph Conrad. Yet this was not due to
indifference or neglect. It was only the British
way. An event which would have been featured
in our journalism was there by preference an-
nounced to the world in the very briefest and
simplest of notices. People were not gathering or
talking about it and to all appearances they did
not know. But if you spoke with anybody about

41

it, a policeman or a clerk or a shopkeeper or any-
one in the hotel, you discovered that everybody
knew. It was the English way and who shall say
that it was not a better way?

I do not think that most people had any idea
what Joseph Conrad's religion was until there
came the announcement that his wonderful career
had closed. No line in his writings ever suggests
it; his own story of his life "A Personal Record,"
is silent about it; and indeed many of his closest
friends never knew. Shortly before his death I
asked one of his friends, at whose home I had
once visited when Mr. Conrad was also a guest,
and he said that nothing had ever brought the
subject up and he could not tell. Once at this
friend's house when I was talking with Mr. Conrad alone and he was answering with utter freedom any question one chose to ask, it was for a
moment on the tip of my tongue to ask him this
question, but somehow I refrained. As I look
back it seems as if it would not have been in-
delicate to ask it. One can hardly help being
curious about this. I remember how quickly and
cordially Mr. Howells replied that he was a Sweden-
borgian when I asked the question of him. Mr.

Conrad's Polish birth might have suggested an answer to this question, but we had almost ceased to think of him as a Pole and so the public announcement that he would be buried from St. Thomas' Catholic church in Canterbury was for most people the first intimation they ever had of his connection with any communion.

From the quiet, outlying village of Bishopsbourne within sound of Canterbury's bells he was to be brought into the city. It was the second time in three centuries that a great man of letters had ended his days in Bishopsbourne. The first was Richard Hooker of The Ecclesiastical Polity, "the Judicious Hooker," who had courted publicity just as little and loved seclusion just as much as Joseph Conrad did. But his home life had been so tragically different from Conrad's that where the latter could speak of "the even flow of daily life, made easy and noiseless for me by a silent watchful, tireless affection," Hooker had to say to his two friends, Sandys and Cranmer, as they departed from his house because they could stand it no longer and were frankly commiserating him for his domestic unhappiness, "If saints have usually a double share in the miseries of this life, I, that am none, ought not to repine at what my wise Creator hath appointed for me, but labor (as indeed I do daily) to submit mine to his will, and possess my soul in patience and peace."

Mrs. Conrad has told how in all their moves it seemed predestined that they should come back to Kent, but even here they were contemplating one move more. There lies before me the copy of one of Mr. Conrad's letters of the early summer in which he wrote about it: "I haven't done much since you have seen me and, truth to tell, I have not been very well either. Our intention is to leave this house in September, but I must confess that we have not yet found another. All this is very disturbing mentally—and the sense of bodily discomfort of which I am almost never free is not very helpful to literary composition. I will not deny that my spirits suffer from this state of affairs. But I won't enlarge on that, which I regard as a passing phase which must be faced with all the resolution one can muster. We haven't had many visitors here lately and, truth to say, I don't feel very sociably inclined." It was on a day in August when Joseph Conrad went in search of this new home that the summons came.

Some hours before the service at the church I had walked out to the cemetery to lay some flowers at his grave. The great breadths of purple felt covered the surrounding ground beneath the trees. Not a soul was there save a laborer or two working in the distance. Canterbury cemetery is the most sunny and beautiful of resting places and one could wish no pleasanter port after stormy seas. The Church of England people lie at the left, the Nonconformists in the central space and the Roman Catholics at the right, but no visible line separates them and to a stranger the cemetery is one and not three.

The requiem was to be at the little church in Burgate Street just off the main thoroughfare of Canterbury and a few minutes before the hour appointed I went to the church wondering whether it would be possible to enter at all. But there was not a sightseer in the street, no one was looking out of door or window or waiting at the churchyard gate and within the church itself not a person was present. The world-wide interest in Joseph Conrad and his works, the eagerness with which everybody received each little item of added information about him, whether as author or man, seemed so incompatible with the silences and absences of that day. One by one a few people, seemingly the usual parishioners rather than people drawn by interest in the great writer himself, slowly assembled. The kindly and venerable priest, Father Sheppard, entered and himself lighted the candles on the altar and beside the bier. An occasional worshipper came in for private devotions and then withdrew and when at last the bell began its tolling there were perhaps three-score persons present.

Shortly the little procession of the pastor and four acolytes moved up the aisle followed by the bearers with the deep casket borne upon their shoulders, and followed by the two sons, Borys and John, and the men of Mr. Conrad's family or household. After the opening of the office the pastor retired and a younger priest came forth to celebrate the mass, which a few moments later paused for a space while some forgotten element necessary to the ritual was sent for and brought by one of the altar boys. The mass was sung in the appointed portions by a modest choir of four parishioners in the gallery and at its close the pastor returned and said the absolutions. In the midst of the service a group of distinguished-looking men arrived and took their places in the company, which had now considerably increased.

But through all this rite, tender and august at once, one's mind kept dwelling with wonder on this strange career now ended, of which there had hardly been a counterpart in the world. One thought of the rich, mysterious personality, the great gifts, the amazing hazards and experiences of his life and all the turns of fortune and experience and the most amazing of all that he should ever have become a writer. And somehow it was not easy to associate Joseph Conrad with this or any definite ceremony. As the clouds of incense rose around him he seemed so remote from it all. It was easier to connect him with winds and waves and skies, with the elemental and the universal.

Then to the music from Saul the procession moved out into the sunlight. Still there was no crowd in the street, those who happened to be there simply stopped where they were, the butcher boy with his tray or the carter or the shopkeeper

at his door, all baring their heads, and almost un-
noticed the cortège moved out into the thoroughfare.

At the cemetery gates a company of friends
and men of letters who had arrived from London
had gathered and walked behind the casket on
its carriage through the winding paths of the
cemetery. What countenances Britain does produce! I recall the word of a radical clergyman of
our country who could scarcely find a good word
to say of any of the ancient communions, who,
returning from a cathedral tour in England, said
that though he had no love for the Church of
England he had never seen such glorious countenances as it produced.

The crucifer stood at the head of the grave
and the acolytes beside him with the candles,
whose light the bright sun had put out but the
ever gracious symbolism of them remained. The
priest stood in the pathway at the foot of the
grave and a parishioner advanced and gave him
the notes for the intoning and the office began.
Twice he circled the grave, once for the censing
and once for the sprinkling and then handed the
aspersorium to Mr. Conrad's younger son, John,

who from it shook a few drops upon his father's casket. Up out of the midst of the sonorous Latin it came as a surprise to hear the familiar words "Joseph Conrad" as the priest called him by name. It was a gentle and kindly service, there was no pomp, it was homely and familiar, not as being the burial of a man of fame but just one more of the sons of men coming to rest at last in mother earth.

Then came the pause when the hundred or more people stood silent for a few moments of reverence and thought. Across the turf stood that other writer of the sea, Mr. Jacobs, and at a little distance the new Dean of Canterbury, the successor of Alford and Farrar and Wace, almost the youngest of deans, whose appointment had given so great satisfaction to the thousands of friends he had made all over Christendom by the charm and wisdom and grace with which he had so long borne the office of Chaplain to the Archbishop. But there was a special sense of fitness and completeness in the presence there of the one who may be said to have been Joseph Conrad's discoverer. It was Mr. Garnett, and it was he who was the reader for the publishers to whom Captain Conrad had sent his first manuscript, "Almayer's Folly." It was he who first felt the presence of a great gift and went to seek out the person who had sent it, surprised beyond measure to find its author a sea-captain. And Conrad has told us that so little was his heart set upon a literary career that if this had been rejected he would never have written any more.

One by one we walked forward and looked down into the grave and upon the silver cross with the drops of absolution still glistening upon it. Then the company dispersed.

I went into a distant part of the cemetery wishing to return after all was concluded and obtain if possible for two distant friends of Mr. Conrad a picture of his resting place after it should be covered with flowers. But when I came back the great wreaths and sprays still lay upon the ground. And as I waited the custodian of the place politely asked me if I would not arrange them myself as I would like them to be. I looked down upon the names of those who had sent them: Ada and John Galsworthy, Sir Hugh Clifford, Muirhead Bone, the etcher, whom a little more than a year before I had watched one evening as he was in the act of etching a portrait of Mr. Conrad. One card bore a noble sentiment from "Nostromo"; but perhaps most beautiful and touching of all was the great wreath from "the Staff at Oswalds," the household servants who must have known better than most the deep kindliness of the man.

Canterbury's latest pilgrim had come home. The circuit he had traversed had been one of the widest and strangest, lacking no single element of romance. Beginning with Poland and the Ukraine, covering the South Seas, reaching to the Congo and the Indies, it was England all the time on which his heart was patiently set. He had hastened nothing, he had forced no circumstances save those first ones when as a boy he had beat down all opposition against his being a sailor and had betaken himself to the sea. And after that he had taken whatever came. His life was singularly complete in all but years. Besides his marvelous writing he had added a great soul and a great personality to the ever-growing riches of our English world. Though one might conceivably find difficulties in Joseph Conrad's writings, while others are drawn captive by him from the very start, none can fail to be fascinated with

51

A BURIAL IN KENT

Conrad the man. And now to all of Canterbury's treasures there is added one quiet place of pilgrimage the more.

BIBLIOGRAPHICAL
NOTES

BIBLIOGRAPHICAL NOTES

A BOOKSELLER, in whose well-lined shop I had spent many hours of profitable browsing, persuaded me to let him send a set of Conrad's first editions to my house in the country on the chance that the author might be in a mood to gratify the desire of one of his customers for that possession, sought after by all collectors—a signed set. Upon unpacking the books and arranging them on a shelf, I noticed, with amazement, that the anonymous owner had inserted in each volume a typed slip asking a question about the book or one of its characters, which he evidently expected Conrad to answer. The sheer audacity of this enterprise took my breath away, and when later I brought it to Conrad's attention he marvelled at the impertinence and said he could not think of gratifying such curiosity. Then with that affectionate thoughtfulness which so endeared him to his friends, he said: "But, my dear fellow, you have never asked me to sign *your* set, and I should like to do so if you don't mind. Where is it?" I pointed it out and left him to his own devices while I attended to some duties out of doors. When I returned an hour later I found him busy at the library table with books piled in stacks all about him. "Do you know," he exclaimed, "some of this fellow's questions are very acute and pertinent and a few are very acute and impertinent; I have decided to answer them as they deserve." And he actually spent over an hour writing in the different volumes. Before returning the books, I made copies of the questions and of Conrad's answers and they are here reproduced, as are also the less interesting, but to me priceless, inscriptions he wrote in my own books.

E. L. A.

ოოო

ALMAYER'S FOLLY

Query. A situation unrelieved in its tropical intensity. Was it consciously or unconsciously that the hard, brilliant effect of the description was achieved? An author's first attempt at effect, if worked in consciously, usually fails; and there is no doubt as to the artistic success of Almayer.

Answer. My very first attempt at writing, as related in "A Personal Record."

NOTES

AN OUTCAST OF THE ISLANDS

Query. Almayer's grudge against Willems is founded on his bringing of the Arabs into the river. Is it not true that in the tropics sensation and reaction are reduced to more elemental terms and personal grudges are founded on more intimate happenings?

Answer. This acute remark is perfectly true.

ᘖᘖᘖ

THE NIGGER OF THE NARCISSUS

Query. In the language that Wait uses, there is a superiority that does not quite lend itself to the character. Was James Wait a sailor or not? Is it generally understood that the West Indian negro has a better command of English than the United States negro, through association with the cultured English of the islands?

Answer. J. Wait is quite authentic.

By this book I stand or fall as an artist in prose. My first "storm-piece."

57

Delaware Valley
College Library

TYPHOON

Query. To create out of oneself a storm such as "Typhoon" depicts is a tour-de-force indeed. How much is due to verbal mastery and how much recollection of many storms is a delicate point. A fine eclecticism is needed to describe one sunset to fit all, or paint a stage drop that will be representative. Is it in the personality of Mac Whirr that the tour-de-force seems to lose itself and the whole thing to become almost as a piece of one's own vital experience?

Answer. Quite correct. Directly I got the conception of MacWhirr I had my story.
My 2nd "storm-piece."

ᕫᕫᕫ

WITHIN THE TIDES

Query. Do you think that, regardless of the injunctions of art, truth or life, people caught in the toils of passion are more likely to give themselves away than to reflect upon or qualify their actions? In the case of Felicia and Geoffrey for instance.

Answer. I did not mean "giving themselves away"

in that sense at all, if your question originates in
a statement in the author's note to that vol. of
tales. Otherwise you may be right.

୭୭୭

TALES OF UNREST

Query. Stories based on experience need a conscious artistry weaving them into a perfect whole,
and sometimes it is difficult to determine how
much was real and how much imaginative, especially after a lapse of time. How much of actual
incident went into these, especially "Karain"?

Answer. "Outpost" built round an actual fact
in a spirit of scorn.

"Karain" was suggested by odd bits of various
stories heard at different times.

"Return" a conscious attempt at mere virtu-
osity.

"Lagoon" a piece of emotional prose.

୭୭୭

THE MIRROR OF THE SEA

The book of the first 20 years of my life after
the early youth period. Can not talk about it.

NOSTROMO

Query. The whole character of "our man" is in keeping with the conception as outlined elsewhere, but is it so simple as all that? Did not the conception grow as the book got bigger with many returns to fill in and round out?

It is hard to say, for what seems like an interpolation may only have been due to interruption, and the regaining of a fresh slant upon the incidents as a whole, on taking hold of the pen again.

Answer. Product of two years of steady work and continuous steady grip on my subject.

ගගග

'TWIXT LAND AND SEA

THE SECRET SHARER.

Query. 1. Will you give the name of the owner and the ship on which this story is based?

A SMILE OF FORTUNE.

2. What was the genesis of this tale?

FREYA OF THE SEVEN ISLES.

3. What is the exact location of this story?

Answer. 1. I wonder what right you think you have to ask such questions? The name was H. Simpson & Sons. The vessel was *The Otago.* Neither the firm nor the vessel exists now.

2. It would take too long to tell.

3. The exact locality of that story is named in the tale.

☙☙☙

VICTORY

Query. Who was the personality that served as a background for the figure of Axel Heyst? He is too vivid to be pure fiction yet he is too complete to be actual.

Answer. For such inquiries I must refer the inquirer to my prefaces as printed in the "de luxe" edition published by Doubleday, Page & Co.

☙☙☙

CHANCE

Query. From all indications both in solidity of plot, interest of character portrayal, and the demand upon the emotions of the average reader this ought to have been a considerable success. Do the facts bear up to this judgment?

Answer. My first "selling" success.

ରରର

A PERSONAL RECORD

Query. In "Chance" the emotions attendant upon the experience of getting a master's certificate are very vividly described. But did Mr. Conrad actually obtain his first command in London or was it in the colonies?

Answer. First command (age 29) was obtained abroad. (See "The Shadow Line.")
All my examinations were passed in London, as related in this book.

ରରର

LORD JIM

Query. The underlying temperament of Lord Jim is acute self-consciousness, due to a characteristic pose of desiring to appear well in men's eyes and the weakness derived from too much introspective thinking. Its artistic triumph lies in the perfect alignment of these two actuating motives in the life of man. But how much of this was wrought into the calibre of the man and how much brought about by incident needs a nice balancing. Did he deserve a better end or did he not?

Answer. I did my best for him. He was one of us.

ᘒᘒᘒ

THE RESCUE

Query. In the trilogy comprising "The Outcast of the Islands," "Almayer's Folly" and "The Rescue," the figure of Captain Linguard looms prodigiously and yet in the notes there is no, or barely any, mention of him. He may not be important to development but he seems to be a sort of "deus ex machina" that misses fire (to mix metaphors). His is a curious nature, a mixture of Billy Hayes and Mission (the French Utopian idealist of Madagascar). Is he a compound or an actual figure?

Answer. I knew both the nephews of the late Captain Linguard, who died in the early 'eighties. He is a creation. I made only use of his name. For the rest the experience of 20 years of life— my life—went to make him what he is in the book.

๑๑๑

NOTES ON LIFE AND LETTERS

Query. Do you think that Paderewski's tenure of office in Poland had the success that was anticipated?

Answer. I do not know what sort of success was anticipated for Paderewski.

๑๑๑

THE ARROW OF GOLD

Query. Is not the person referred to in "The Arrow of Gold" as "the writer's childhood friend" the same as served for the figure of Antonia in "Nostromo"? This book seems to be the most intimate of the author's books, discounting even the "Mirror of the Sea" and "A Personal Record." There is a quality of taking the reader into con-

64

fidence, which after all, is the surest way to seize upon his attention. It gives out a more complete record of life and adventure both of body and mind. There are also intimations scarcely tangible perhaps of other figures and events met before—subtle recollections bringing one nearer to the living reality which is one of the thrills of reading and living in books. "The Arrow of Gold" makes this appeal effectively through the notes bringing in the personal touch and awakening recollection. There are disclosures that no one is entitled to ask, even of an author, but since he has already "itched with confession" resulting in an incomparable body of writing, a few words on this point of recollection would not be out of place.

Answer. I regret I can say nothing more intimate. As a matter of fact all that would bear telling is told in the book. I am delighted with the inquirer's appreciation.

ର୍ତ୍ତର୍ତ୍ତ

UNDER WESTERN EYES

Query. The old teacher of languages has a literary affinity with the Marlow of other books.

BIBLIOGRAPHICAL

Each author has some idiosyncracy, a vein of development that he follows in his working of the mine of thought. Is this trait, as one might call it, conscious or unconscious?

Answer. The "western eyes" are the eyes of the old teacher of languages. That is why he is there.

ରରର

A SET OF SIX

Query. Though the fact and the subsequent development of the story may bear little in common, it is curious to note the change of tenor in their relation. In "Il Conde," for instance, where does the old man leave off and Conrad begin?

Answer. The story is bare truth. The psychology of the narrator is my invention but the personality *did* suggest it.

ରରର

THE SECRET AGENT

Query. Its genuineness as an artistic piece of work cannot be doubted when one considers the author's own background and heredity.

66

How much of this background colored the impulse? How did the connotation of the words "anarchist" "nihilist" serve to awaken thought and build up an edifice of imaginative impulse?

Answer. My origin had nothing to do with this story. Never knew an anarchist in my life. Story built on an anecdote.

∂∂∂

YOUTH

Query. An all-too-wonderful thing to be accepted as an actual experience, but rather as an emotion recollected in tranquillity, which, according to Wordsworth, is one of the elements of great poetry. As a poem then it is authentic. The feelings as described by Marlow had as a background the whole romance of the East India Company and the 18th Century nabobs. Could it be expected of a youth of eighteen to have this?

Answer. I do not know what may be "expected of a youth of 18." I was twenty when I was 2nd officer of the *Palestine* and 38 when I wrote that story, which is a strictly personal experience. As to the prose in which it is embodied it is even more strictly "personal" than the experience.

ΘΘΘ

FALK

Query. Is it the ruthlessness of those who feel actuated by a moral code, or the delicacy of the moral code that brings out the brutality of man's desire? A nice point which Falk seems to be on the point of deciding, but does not.

Answer. A certain brutality in self-preservation may be allied to innate moral delicacy.

See author's note (preface) to the volume in the limited edition.

ΘΘΘ

ROMANCE

Middle of the book almost entirely mine.

ΘΘΘ

THE INHERITORS

Very little writing in this book is mine. Hueffer

practically held the pen. The discussions were endless.

ᔥᔥᔥ

AT SEA WITH JOSEPH CONRAD

Don't know anything of this book except that I permitted Sutherland to write and publish it.

INSCRIPTIONS

ALMAYER'S FOLLY

" 'It has set at last' said Nina to her mother." . .

(*p.* 193.)

TYPHOON

". . . an everlasting to-morrow."

(*p.* 304, *last words of* "*To-morrow.*")

THE NIGGER OF THE NARCISSUS

By these pages I stand or fall.

WITHIN THE TIDES

". . . all sorts of courage except the courage
to run away."

(*p.* 48, "*Planter of Malata.*")

TALES OF UNREST

". . . a world of illusions."

(*p.* 297, *end of* "*The Lagoon.*")

INSCRIPTIONS

THE MIRROR OF THE SEA
The book of my first life.

NOSTROMO
My greatest creative effort.

'TWIXT LAND AND SEA
"Ever since the sun rose I had been looking ahead."

(First words of "A Smile of Fortune.")

VICTORY
". . . Murmured with placid sadness, 'Nothing.'"

(p. 415, end words.)

CHANCE
My first selling success.

LORD JIM
"'Man is amazing, but he is not a masterpiece' he said . . ."

(p. 221.)

THE ARROW OF GOLD
"I live by my sword."

(p. 8, Captain Blunt.)

71

INSCRIPTIONS

YOUTH

". . . into the heart of an immense darkness."

(p. 182.)

THE SHADOW LINE

Not a ghost story, as some critics would have it, but the actual story of my first command.

UNDER WESTERN EYES

This book was much read in Russia before the Great War.

THE SECRET AGENT

". . . in the street full of men."

(p. 442, last words.)